WILD A

Michael Hamburger

Wild and Wounded

SHORTER POEMS 2000–2003

ANVIL PRESS POETRY

Published in 2004
by Anvil Press Poetry Ltd
Neptune House 70 Royal Hill London SE10 8RF
www.anvilpresspoetry.com

Copyright © Michael Hamburger 2004

This book is published with financial assistance
from The Arts Council of England

Designed and set in Monotype Ehrhardt by Anvil
Printed and bound in England
by Cromwell Press, Trowbridge, Wiltshire

ISBN 0 85646 371 X

APOLOGY

If here, dear dedicatee, I hide your name
It's from a dual shame:
At repetition: always it's been the same,
So near you are that far, the knot undone,
Ocean and law dividing us, we were one;
And difficulties with grammar now, with tense,
With mood, with person, case – and, yes, the sense.
Most proper nouns, grown improper, I forget,
The daily like the unprecedented scene
Slithers into a past that is not yet.
Therefore loose bounds I set
Against this dropping-out of place, of time,
Resort to obvious rhyme
Merging what has been, is, in will-have-been.
Else the undying dead
Inhabitants of my head
Would there crowd out the living – but for you.
How could our rhyme be new?
Half-waking, half-asleep,
Pensioner of a less mendacious age,
Plain implements I keep,
Laughable scythe, fixed hand-saw, stone-chipped spade,
Inherited hammer that drives home my rage –
All proven, strongly made
To outlast the need, the use, as lovers do.

ACKNOWLEDGEMENTS

Some of these poems have appeared in the following
periodicals:

Agenda, Babel (Germany), *Decision* (Germany),
Europäische Ideen (Germany), *Irish Pages* (Belfast),
*Leviathan Quarterly, London Magazine, MenCard,
Neue Rundschau* (Germany), *Poetry Ireland, P N
Review, Poetry Review, The Shop* (Ireland), *Stand,
Text + Kritik* (Germany) and *The Threepenny Review*
(USA).

A few of them were included in a reading recorded
for the Poetry Archive, on a CD to be released in
May 2004.

CONTENTS

III

IV

I

REDUNDANT EPITAPHS

(for friends not named)

I

Night now,
Returned from Egypt, Thrace,
Mexico, Scythia, Tibet,
Wherever by tenants of stellar space-time
Tombs with the things of day
Were furnished, for the dark,
Night crops were eaten, night sculptures carved
By those who deferred to darkness,
Like swallows homed to it, diving,
Built the best homes, the surest
To distract the vicarious few
From the leisure not long but limitless
Of their souls' before and after;
Theirs too, the countless unnamed
Who on daybeds of rock lay down
To rest wrenched limbs from labour.

Yes, light they loved, darkly,
When with gold and jewels they decked
The illustrious, illumined,
Light's play on surfaces,
Facets, fibres, flesh,
Colours invisible
But for light's breaking, rejection
Of the waves not received.
From the more durable dark
Gold, jewels had issued
And for darkness again
Were walled up, in unknowing.

2

Night now,
Advent of frozen rebirth,
The blue-green, the blood-red radiance
Wiped off the western sky
And by morning moonshine no more
Than negatives, black on white, greyish,
Spectral the spectrum's whole range.

Blinded, maimed, spent,
He who'd fought and suffered it
Waited, longed for night
To absolve, absorb him,
Take back the contours, colours
Retained in memory's darkroom,
Mend him once and for all.

Night cased in metal struck
This other who slowly had gathered
Fractions, refractions of light
From the things of day, darkened,
Lovingly had composed them,
He the quick taker of snapshots
Against the sundown dazzle,
The murk that blots it below.
Then white,
The days' air hazed, opaque,
White on black, equalized,
Skeletal twigs, residual stalks
Stark on the snowsheet's blankness.

3

Night now.
A dog whines for his lost companion,
Mentor and keeper who lately, recalled by pity
Broke off secluded work,
For the sick dog's healing crossed land and sea.
Without nightlight of stars or candle the dog lives on,
In absence beyond recall.

While eyes hunger, hands move,
Human love defies it,
With tinsel decks the tree,
With birdfeed the garden table,
Exchanges tokens, gifts,
Brightnesses even after the funeral service,
Against loss, abeyance;
To the habit of selfhood, business always unfinished,
Emptier years makes its way.
To more light again, to more making?
A dog's love denies it.

4

Night, then,
Capacious enough to contain
The quirks and quiddities
Alive in sunlight, ever,
Reflecting the light or hidden,
Known or unknown,
Knowing, unknowing,
Traceable yet or bare
As gravestones the weathers washed.
To the open new grave a robin came down,
An icy wind blew
On the bird safe there among the living
And those more truly levelled
Than sunlight lets creatures be –
All reduced, irreducible there,
In one darkness stood and lay.

DETAINED

I

Opening my wardrobe door
I'm back at a roadside lodging
In Ireland once, the location overlaid,
Where such a door opened
On a lost husband's clothes,
Love's loyalty clinging,
The sepulchral smell.

Older, newer, my own
Belong to the parts
Played here or there on stages dismantled,
Remote from me as the widow's patter
Served with breakfast to passing guests
After so dank a meeting –
Even the buried man's razor
Left on the bathroom shelf still.

2

A whiff of the staleness only,
Now, in a house full of relics,
Their clearance near, and one distance merges
Daylight landmarks in night's.
Mortal throughout a cold spring, dark summer
The wild and the rarer flowers open,
This Dutch elm survives where it was not planted,
This pampered peach-tree, robinia, larch and linden,
One thirsty alder too –
Storms, rising water, fungus, blight have unleafed.

3

Dreaming, I read a request
From a critic redundant or dead
That I respond to his response
To a poem I cannot own,
Strange to me though it bears my name.
Never collected. Never published?
The silt of earlier dreams has bedded
Dubious books of mine no copy of which
Ever surfaced, my best.
Did I, then, write it, this fragment
Beyond my comprehension?
And searching another man's room,
Could I unlock my belongings?

A half-way house it proved, anyone's,
Its contents claimed by lenders
No less forgotten than words called his or mine.

The scene shifted, dialogue subsided
Into the silence it had issued from.

4

Now that weathers, day after day,
Flee from abandoned seasons,
Frantic clouds rush across
Intermissions of cancerous rays,
Must love unlearn its clinging,
Its labour cease?

For woodwind music, the high and low,
Caged raspberry canes were let loose to rampage,
A thicket pasture for birds,
Buddleia left to spread
For flimsier wings whose illumination
Held clues to a cryptic script.

Who'll read it now, the half-wilderness
We made and did not make?
Maintain that equipoise
Or in white haze of flowering ground elder,
Pale hemp agrimony cluster, meadowsweet
Missed by bindweed's clinch
Trace the lost garden in outlines almost erased?

                    5

'Married?', he asks, the turnkey at the gate,
As we prepare to leave,
Detaining us with conundrums less angelic
Than bureaucratic, some logo on his lapel –
A part-time stand-in, he says, happening to be on duty
For gabbled, garbled messages I must translate
Into their meaning:
                    'Emigrants? Yes, confirmed.
From a subverted state, notorious.
Innocence, you pronounce it? Lost to you? Not attested.
Asylum needed? Routine, mates. Not so fast!
Look back or forward, it makes no difference,
Within, outside these bounds . . .

If it's judgement you're after,
Somewhere a court is in session – in flux? –

High up, they don't tell us, where . . .
Before you did, your lilies gave up,
Neutered by snail or slug,
Swallows made for their mud-nests and vanished,
One cuckoo's one call was rumoured to have been heard . . .
Then a young grass-snake coiled in a flowerpot saucer –
Compost had hatched it, so close to its origin –
Back here at last, as fondly was welcomed
As the frogs you tended, herons only had gulped . . .
Did Francis and his Claire
Weld the plucked apple again to the bough?
Ponder that while you wait . . .
Frustrated, are you, glum?
Well, there is one thing more
I'm competent to – er – remind you of:
Sooner or later you'll get there,
The other place where quotas are unknown,
Its multiple dimensions so capacious
All it accomodates that ever was,
All selfed, all selfless sorts that ever were,
Up to the stars extinguished,
Stars with no shape yet, let alone name or site . . .
Making of that what you can,
Curb your impatient lust for certainties
Which process will dissolve, the never to be computed . . . '

6

On the salt shore, in sand, in dry shingle
Horned poppy finds food for a purest yellow,
Seakale oasis for waves of glaucous lush leaves.
Where we sit, she and I,
The greeny-black wall of a yew has compacted
Our decades here, deciduous, its infant years.

Hidden until the air
Invited them to circle,
Their wings could cut the currents,
No turbulence blur their cries,
House martins, swifts have bred,
Now mend a summer, late,
By making visible
Their homing, their departure.

This rustling, ruffling of leafage is warblers
Leaf-coloured almost when twiglets reversed show white.

A flitting has turned into stillness. The clocks have stopped.

DIMINUENDO

So long has the evening primrose lit
Darkening air, the dusk in leaves
That invisible almost it glimmers
As though duration like recurrence dimmed
Sun-yellow stored in those lamps
A mind could read by, seeing to construe
Late in the day, month, year
When wind-blown, limp, verbena
Grounds its mauve-purple, the foil;

Low too, white colchicum,
Half-hidden cyclamen
Taunt with untimely spring
The worker wearying
Of soil's cryptography
Whom, ripe pears picked, the tree
Shocks with a twig in blossom.
Profuse perplexity
Soon will strike him dumb.

No need for snow
To repossess
The more grown less:
Gardener, let go,
New seedlings urge
Whose features merge
In afterglow.

MUTED SONG

Darkening days of the year
Before the solstice, Advent
In the ripped grove's detritus.
Wind from the Urals, cruel.
One last campanula's mauve
Bravely, silently peals,
Gazania, dipping, flaunts
Flame petals, African, still.
Under stripped apple-trees
Ungathered fruit, the yellow,
Russet or crimson, lies,
Dole to the songbirds, deer.

It's nightfalls only let
A half-remembered light
Dapple cloud-leaded skies,
The star in hiding glitter.
Chilled the root fibres raise
To buds their sustenance
And numb limbs dance
To rhythms that absence beats.
A nearly deaf man sings
Come, that we waiters praise
Who serve expectancy,
The always never-yet.

WILD AND WOUNDED

I

Visit or visitation, when in frost
A heron descends to the garden pond
For any snack, late frog or goldfish fry,
Frustrated by the cover's netting stands
A monument to hunger, motionless?

So it has always been.
But on the snow-flecked lawn
As never yet in twenty-six winters here
A swan sat, whiter, hissed when we fed him bread,
For two days barely shifted, though he grazed
Within his lithe neck's radius,
Calmer than we were after another death –
Until he made to rise,
Dragging one leg, a wobbling majesty
Not come by choice, for refuge
From riveret pasture puddled now and iced,
Crash-landed, gashed while in flight or fight:
A casualty, a case,
Therefore to be removed, hospitalized.

2

Meddling is human, Adam said, and Cain,
Remembrance mortal too. The haunting ceases.
Get out your guest-book, then,
Your cenotaph of the fallen, who knows where,
No matter if incomplete:
For winter, jack-snipe, furrowing, red-legged partridge,
Fieldfare and redwing, song and missel thrush,
Three kinds of other rank sparrows, noted when they
    were gone,
The whole long field mottled with plovers daily,
Dusk marked by barn-owl's passing
And for top brass marsh harrier's whirl at prey.
Oh, and the swallows, martins more than missed
For their low muttering, wilderness brought home.

3

No loss to them, merged in their time unmeasured,
Nameless identity
That suffering, maimed, wants nothing but to be
Or perish, so humble their indifference.
Roused from complaisance, looking, walking, we
Clash with an empty cage
Which, wildering, we, for our not their defence
Blast in self-injuring rage
At absence, ours to feel, of trapped lives treasured:
End of an age, our age.

4

The tamed no less, the petted, the still tended,
Our cultivars driven wild:
Clenched rose in January, primrose and violet
Amid the aconites, growth without rhyme or season
By the mad weathers tricked, beguiled:
A warm breeze after hurricane, frost and rain
That seemed unending, flooded the kitchen floor,
Those weathers in our doings, in our minds.
When friends and strangers met for this New Year
The small-talk halted, ripped by small detonations –
Of course, the firework rockets in the street,
Defiant celebrations,
Larger explosions imminent, not here,
Too near the fission works long obsolete.

5

Dreaming, I see my father sixty-three years dead
Come to my work-room where engrossed, engaged
I ask the walking wounded
To wait a little in the sitting-room
Before I join him there.
But then it's travels, devious and drawn-out,
Uncertainties, delays.
At a forgotten house
I see my mother opening some back pantry door,
Her who died forty years later,
Remind her who I am. She seems preoccupied,
Almost fades out, the scene – a home? – suspended.
Perhaps, though, turning, less absorbed, she whispered:
'Come back when *you* have died.'

6

Frost has returned, rime to the swans' terrain
Beside the riveret
Where, whiter, distant, a family crops and wanders,
Even or odd, symmetrical, incomplete.
I'll count no heads now, lines or syllables
To fix this whiter whiteness quivering.

FALLEN

Whenever, clearing in my garden,
I have to lop or weed,
Hidden but near this robin cries: No! No!
'Gamekeeper are you of the status quo
Long become ante? You, a bird that preys
On earthworms gulped down whole, on living seed?
When you have changed your ways
I'll put away my implements, desist.'
Yet he's no hypocrite, in my heart I know:
Under my breath I beg his pardon,
My fellow conservationist.

MEMORIAL

Raincloud, hailcloud, snowcloud behind them,
So fast the north-easterly drives
That no sky can cohere:
Against black horizon
For a minute, stark
In full rays broken through
The beech-tree long barkless
Stands as never when leaved,
All golden its wrecked limbs.

SUMMER YET AGAIN

Wake up, the flowers are flying past
You slow-coach getting slower,
Limbs of the tree most relied on
Surreptitiously dying,
All the kinds fulfilled in passing
And for you the passing too fast.
Will immobility
Lend you eyes that can see?

Yes, inwards: whole streets demolished,
Faces undone, empires, orders dissolved,
Locations, names mislaid, cities flown over, by-passed.
If longer than our landmarks, loves we last
Into a dream we sink,
Late and early commingled, living and dead,
Round-bellied nightmare of searches, losses
Rides the reposing head.

Wake to the sleep, then, of selfless things,
Out of time, duration,
Beyond your human mind.
From the willow's peeled boughs a dove is flying,
A marsh harrier from stillest air
Stoops for predation,
Old roses have climbed new skeletons, entwined.
Dream those, impartially.

THE DOG-DAYS INTERRUPTED

When in hottest July
Thunder rips the sky,
Blown grey clouds block the white,
Not quite burnt out a few red poppies loom
Among the fallen that wait
For after-life, prostrate,
Short showers too late
For all save the long-suffering to bloom,
Winds mix the season's light,
Mixed currents bring relief
To the still clinging leaf,
To fruit still filling, flower to come,
Myrtle moons budding in their darkness yet
And human sharer, grim
Before that interim.
But now the butterflies
From near-abeyance rise
Mingled, the early, late,
The commonest, the rare –
A feverish consummation
Almost too rich for buddleia-searching eyes.
This whitethroat, more inferred
Than either seen or heard,
Flits in to fit the word.
Thanks to the thunder only, winnowing,
A wane has mended, a clash has purged the air.

II

II

'AN EMBASSADOR IS AN HONEST MAN, SENT TO LIE ABROAD FOR THE GOOD OF HIS COUNTREY'

(Izaac Walton's rendering of Sir Henry Wotton's album entry, a translation more accurate than the original.)

A towering pun it could have been without
The *universal language*'s unambiguity –
A capital pun when Latinized out of doubt,
But for an age poetic, from the King down
Who at this liberty must fret and frown,
Then with a smile forgave it, being free.
(Poetry tells the truth, ambiguously.)
Love made the difference, magnanimity.

Now lies, like charity, begin at home,
Down from the top to little money-makers,
Witless the lot, the sellers and the takers,
The public realm redundant as our Dome.

Where sparrows die, so will the sparrow-hawk.
Puns lose their point where all is double-talk.

SKETCHES TOWARDS
AN IMPOSSIBLE PORTRAIT

Jonathan, Jonathan – who ever called him so
Save the soon distant mother, and again
Of all his patrons the most powerful
For a few years, making him what?
A servant or familiar
Whom his bare surname riled, in any mouth.

Leave out his eyes
Lest you presume a verisimilitude,
Tell what can not be told:
Warmed-up historical stew, however strained,
Left-over tittle-tattle.

But, busiest, nightly did he not unbutton,
Unperiwig his loneliness,
In plain vernacular ramble, chat
For either, neither of the women dear
To Presto, dearest when they were not near?
With one as chaperone,
The other his white wife,
Or pupil-mistress or spinster-friend?
Yes, and concealed from both a third
Who'd call him 'not to be known'
And die of knowing that.

Meanwhile he politicked,
Nameless in Grub Street, feared in the ministries
For terrible integrity, his ghoulish wit,
Never quite used there, never quite rewarded:

Unknowable everywhere
Behind the soundbites and the puns
That were the spice of sociability,
Price of subsistence, dinners he endured
Whose health was walking and the plainest fare;
Himself a growler, day after day
Solicited among 'sad dogs' and 'puppies'
All welcome to hospitable disdain,
Though some, the needy, might be honest, meaning
More honest than the smoother ones;

Walked, walked the streets of London and beyond,
Steadfast when threatened by the Mohock slashers,
Against the surfeit, against the giddiness
That in his rented rooms beset him,
Giddiness of the age, a grossness tugging
Downward its finery, good sense grown lumpish,
Means twisted from their ends:
Fewer beheadings in affairs of State,
The more corruption – the more babies eaten?
A roundabout of interest interchanged,
Flogged body dividends
And conscience-alms, cold charity's tax of coins.

Could he be other than what it let him be?
Whig-Tory, English-Irish patriot,
Pining for what? His willows, cherry-trees,
Trout in clean water, his own poor canal's
Back in a humble parish,
Lost, irreducible simplicity?
Grieved for the death of anyone not preferred,
Stranger, half-intimate or enemy,
For living losers put in the loathed word.

'No poet', his cousin Dryden said:
Mistrusted music, verses that run free.
Doctor, he did not teach,
Militant churchman, was not moved to preach,
Rarely disposed to pray
Unless in private – in his little language
Of harsh and hectoring tenderness cut short?
The dutiful Dean's? Gruff satirist's? Pamphleteer's?
None of them fit for worship or for praise.

Don't look for those eyes now. Look away.

One eye swelled up to the size of an egg or heart –
A truly Swiftian tumor,
Last product of his humour? –
And he, deserted, deaf, maimed, maddened, maddening
    cried:
'I am what I am, I am what I am' –
Blasphemous in extremity, self-deified?
Gulliver a Prometheus, masked? Now stripped to the pride
Hellishly punished even in pagan Greece? –
Were it intelligible, he to be sounded, known.

Best let such ill alone.
Leave off your prying. Leave him in peace.

THE ALIENATION OF JOHN CLARE

1

In France it meant madness, *aliénation mentale*.
With a twist Dr Marx turned it social-economic.
Under one system, would-be Marxist,
Political deviants were treated as mental cases,
Under another, anti-Marxist,
Mental cases were culled like cattle, slaughtered
In the cause of eugenics, long practised by cattle-breeders.
So add a third connotation,
Scientific madness, akin to the bureaucratic,
Subservient to money-madness
If on its pay-roll, or purely, autonomously mad
As logic, theory, administration, method become
When insulated from those or that they work upon –
The madness that moves the manipulators of genes.

2

Yes, yes, the peasant poet briefly raised
Above his station
Till dropped below it, genially,
By patrons, publishers, public by then diverted
From the diversion they could once afford;
Put away twice, exiled to Sodom, Hell
Before the terminal disposal freed him –
Now into classlessness, granted him because dead,
Late, very late, even claimed for the nation,
Promoted to London where, alive, he'd learnt:
Celebrity itself was alienation,

At least for him
Whose health and wealth had fed on trespassing
From mindless drudgery on land enclosed
Into residual 'native wilds', nature to him,
To make it common again, this truant poacher poet.

3

Memory broke in him, the riverbed
Which links the source, pre-natal, to the sea,
Once dug by it, the course of energy,
Curriculum of flux, identity.
Blocked by a dam, those waters in his head
Spread out of sequence: living and dead,
The girl refused him and the woman married,
Mary the might-have-been, made his in Heaven,
Long-suffering Martha, mother of their seven,
A whirlpool mixed. In it time tarried,
The current, now rotated, now reversed,
Eroded selfhood. Somewhere poetry,
Home of the homeless, dispensary of stress,
Retained its hold on one who was not he.
That rhyme could chime there still became the worst
Of his estrangements, worse than the separation
From all belonging, save in timelessness,
Real wildflower, pooty, from imagination,
Words from their substance, loved ones from his care,
Mind from the muscles with nothing more to do.
And stirred again, from stupor, well he knew,
Too clearly, what had severed Clare from Clare.

REST ON THE FLIGHT

(Schiphol)

If the winter sun shines,
Even smoking's permitted,
The first 'plane was not late,
There was no frantic rush from one gate to the distant
    other,
The connecting flight already due to take off,
It's the idyll of anywhere-nowhere
In transit between the engagement met
And home again, home,
Thanks alone to a plastic beaker,
Tea-bag of something called China or Indian,
Synthetic milk in a capsule,
Water still, hot and wet,
Respite, sheer luxury
Of sitting unbelted, unjostled, sipping.

And the terrorists, were they cowed
By the confiscation of nail-file, nail-scissors,
Did they think their bare hands not sufficient
To overpower the pilot, his crew?
Well, they forebore to strike,
Left to fate, mechanical failure,
Themselves and you and me,
This time with time for tea.

MR LITTLEJOY'S BELATED RESPONSE

Roused from a nap, with music on, I hear
The telephone's buzz, no longer loud or clear.
'B.O.B.C.', a voice says. Business call?
Nonplussed I wait. The cipher can't be all.
'Bag of Old Bones Club', he deciphers, pat –
'Oh, yes? And what about it? What of that?'
Then he rings off. The call can not be traced.
Threat? Invitation? Joke in our media's taste?

However meant, a way of putting it:
Only for verse and digging still I'm fit;
Notorious, too, for digging my own grave.
Was he my reader, critic, architrave
Of the blocked doorway, window to a 'world'?
Or random nothingness, boredom's, whirled and hurled
Through electronics grown autonomous
From anyone to anyone, at 'them' by 'us'?

'Go ex-directory', guileless friends advise –
When all is privatized, earth, ocean, skies,
A playground for the enterprise that's free,
Bags of old bones left with no privacy
Until they're coffined or compelled to rest?
No, privately this bone-bag will protest
While there is breath in it, and join no club
Save that of dead bones, thump a dead man's tub.

LETTER TO L. F.

(after the opening of the retrospective exhibition, 2002)

Knowing too well that an artist ought to be
'Like God in his universe,
Present everywhere, visible nowhere'
And recalling those words of Flaubert
From a letter read sixty years back
While too often vainly I fumble
For What-do-you-call-him's identification –
Have we ever met? Do I mix up the faces? Is he he?
I dragged myself all the same
To London with my daughter Claire,
Gasped on the Circle Line,
Slogged past the Houses of Parliament
The length of emptying Millbank
To stand among cocktails we did not come for
In a crowd of important guests,
Owners, I guessed, middlemen, hangers-on
And photographers of the missing person,
Purveyors of the name that you withhold
From paper, canvas, plate.
On that forecourt they smiled and glowered
Before anyone dared to face
The crux of it, Lux, your productions –
Or was it Luchs, the lynx-eyed
When in far-away boyhood we were first acquainted?

You always dared – to see –
Harder work, if less pleasing
Than watery plunges inward,
Impressions, expressions, ingenuities,

Abstractions, fantasies
Though real dreams, real nightmares also
Are corporeal for you as naked flesh,
As the sinks we need though we do not make them.
All of yourself you put into it,
All that you lived and were –
And are not there,

Not in the Paddington where I watched you paint,
Your concentration fed with glucose then,
Present again in this selection
With all the sitters, standers, sprawlers
Most present if they are dead,
Their messages, if we could receive them,
Dotted with hints of a different home:
Oh, a whole pubfull, clubfull from long-lost Soho
And, farther, nearer still, your mother dying, dead
In the St John's Wood of our adolescence –
Down to your features, in youth and age,
A model accessible always, to be brought
Into your media's otherness by meticulous care,
Metamorphosed to the no-time your decades and days affirm.

Few flowers? Few rural idylls, if any?
Yet foliage, rich, like that
Of the African hemp which links
You to my mother from whom
Some fifty years ago
You fetched a potted cutting;
Which, tree-sized now, grows
In your Notting Hill garden,
Your jungle of leaves, interlaced;
Of the prickly thistle you etched –

Not here included
But in my retrospect a telling ghost.

Never mind 'yours' and 'mine', though, friend:
Those pictures filled an absence
With more than token talk ever could.
Let them mutter: 'Godling. Scorned his own celebration.'
Consummation, too, only not for the maker
Wholly engaged in a search that has no end.

AT THE MIXED FARM

Her son it was took off the lid
When, penned, the Arab horses, four,
Were bored, distracted into greed,
But she, the matriarch, who dipped
Deepest into the barley bin
Too near the paling. Age had added
Indifference to the prudence we held dear,
The dignity of her twenty-fourth horse year.
Alone now she waited, silently she dropped.
Chickenfeed did her in, that noble mare.

AT LIVERPOOL STREET STATION

Concrete towers, blocks, rounded, conical, rhomboid,
One a phallic missile, another topped with a crane
Dwarf its bulk to a hulk.
Inside, a two-tier shopping centre
Frames an inhuman space:
In flux, no resting-place
Like that where, a quarter-century back,
The last train missed, through the small hours
Over one cup, one glass I could sit.
If that was hard on the night-shift workers
They served a simple need,
Communal refuge for the assorted fictions
Lived out there nightly, mutable, yet coherent
A stranger could read among
Those homeless by choice, hippy to aging drop-out
And those a schedule stranded.
Many talked there, exchanging their stories
Or, growing weary, could drowse,
Heads drooped on to the tables –
Unless, law and order on night-shift also,
A copper or two with a smile or threat
Less mechanized still than money
Picked on some regular to clear him out
Of those walls demolished now the souls of all of them
    haunt.

POST-PASCHAL, 2003

1

After Good Friday this bitter wind,
Northeasterly, on to dead fibre warmed
Back into bud or leaf, blossom or nucleus.

After the last words, human,
Agony beyond words, too human now
That words are what they use,
Their counterfeit currency
Perverting all they price and sell to trash,
Even the outrage tainted.

To walk immune here in the rising light,
Our pathways quiet, skyline not blasted black
Was to be shamed by the sun's clear shining.

2

What sap stirs now, what moves?
Conquest projected from empty heads
Into long-distance missiles fuelled with money,
Their borrowed billions, unreal estate
That rules the residual real,
Electronically missed their would-be targets
And the limbs of a child exploded.
For bonus, the lying logo affixed
To the cluster bombs of liberation
From home-grown tyranny to its imported replacement
When the ruins and relics, forgotten,
Can be buried in desert sand.

3

Pilate's power was more honest.
The pagan light, nature's,
Left him room for doubt.

Two millennia were needed for this:
Our new age crusaders
Too busy playing golf for their health
To prove what they profess,
Sent out their 'boys' on the thuggish business,
'Girls', too, the new age demanded,
A mere handful of either to be killed or maimed,
Not counting the reporters, men and women,
Closer to true action in this pseudo-war.

Gabriel Rado – did conscience push him
Off the roof not yet unsafe
Or a secret agent less outmoded?

Ask Pilate. And wash your hands.

4

For the next assault, here beginneth the lesson,
Where every beginning is almost the end:

Disarm the enemy who was your friend,
Starve the people, destroy the installations,
Blessed by a cowed, compliant United Nations
You can always by-pass, should it grow brash.
Modernize, modernize! Pretend, pretend!
In that penumbra, Thatcherized New Labour,

Call him potential client, global neighbour
Whom out of deep affinity you bash
Into disorientated frenzy – first.
Then restore order, yours, and do your worst.

5

Ah, but it's words again, weary and wearisome.
The Kingdom has not come.
Satan, the salesman of dominion once,
Laughs at himself: that tempter was the dunce.
This world, distributed, incorporated,
Has been diminished, all the fuss inflated.
The very oil, they say, is running out.
So what was this expenditure about,
Whose mass destruction, whose individual pains,
Propaganda self-dissolving – while confusion reigns?

Silence that mocked could heal it,
Source of water stopped or polluted – drought could reveal it,
Lights that flickered, went out enhance the light that remains.

PLUS ÇA CHANGE ...

A German Vicar's Extempore New Year Prayer, 1883

Dear God and Lord, set bounds to our superfluity
and let boundaries, frontiers become superfluous;
from wives take away the last word
and remind husbands of their first;
give those who govern a better language
and all who speak it a better government;
grant us and our friends more truth
and to the truth more friends;
improve those public servants
who work and fare well enough but produce no welfare;
let those right busy, righteously, also do what is right;
and see to it
that all of us go to Heaven,
but – if that be thy will – not at once.
Amen.

Hermann Kappen, Vicar of St Lamberti, Münster,
and Freeman of that City

III

HOLIDAY TOWN

(Dornbirn, Vorarlberg, Corpus Christi 2001)

I

Peal of bells over the dead streets.
Faint subsidence
Of a brass band far off.
A glint of snow on mountain-tops,
Grey cloud, white cloud, cold air below.
Carpet shops, gimcrack shops,
Even the bakeries closed
As though this day no bread would be eaten
Save that transmuted by sacrifice.

Then not so much sound
Between one Mass and the next
And the June light withheld.
Not a chirp from the sparrows teaching their young to fly
From a high roof's gutter.

When at last the sun breaks through to the valley
Far mountains dissolve in mist.

2

By the flooded footpath along the great lake's shore
Profanely frogs, set back by the weather,
Are in full frenzy of mating-calls.
In tall willows, poplars and birches
Hidden birds are not hushed.

On the German side
A zeppelin old and new
Seems hardly to drift, so slow,
An aerial metallic whale
Basking above the infant Rhine.

3

At the foothill inn
A different music, from Switzerland,
Of alpenhorn players bussed over the border:
Music of loneliness,
Of heights cut off,
Heavy music, slow as the zeppelin,
From tree-branch pipes
Each with the voice of an ancient trunk,
Here in consort for a harmony lumbered.

4

Black, grey, white and silver
At nightfall the sky whirls
Into stillness, the dark.
No voice at all, human, arboreal
Booms from the alps erased.
Still dead, the town waits
For cleansing rain to fall.

INJURED COW

1

The hot spell over, late August turned autumnal
Drove more than twenty of them to stray
From a parched pasture to the rivulet
Steeply, embanked now, so that one was drowned,
Sinking in silt and, silent, looked for too late.

She with a leg wrenched or broken
Perhaps by the rescuing tractor and rope
Day-long, night-long has lain
Close to the bank, unable to lift
The weight bred into her flanks, her udder,
Darkness and sunlight mixed in her patient eyes
As black and white are, dappled, in her hide.

2

If towards dawn we heard
A moaning, lamentation
Her weaned calf it was that cried:
Since her fall she has not stirred
Save when the distant herd
Homed to the byre and milking-shed out of habit –
Not to be milked now, most of them, the dairy trade
Become impracticable, a dead loss.
But for a love of sorts and habit
There'd be no cattle here to graze or breed.

Then, then she strains to rise
And cannot, but the calf
Lopes from the huddle to the mother missed,
Nuzzles and prods, inquisitive,
Yet with a reticence, too, that leaves intact
The larger dignity of her lying-in
Alive, oh, thanks to water, hay provided.

3

Grimness alone sustains the mixed-up farm
In our mixed weather, while that one cow waits
Deep in her silence beyond our talk and pity.

For how much longer? That's been left to nature.
'The farm's economy runs to no vet
Who'd put her down if nature does not raise her,
Though Government offers comfort, compensation
For carcasses that promptly are reported,
Trucked off to the brain autopsy required
By prophylactic measures now in force . . . '
Too late, too late again
For any sort of love or habit, wrenched or broken.

'Yes, milk is needed, processed, meat is eaten.
They haven't learnt yet, have they,
To make a meal of their computed money
Spiced with a potent condiment called "spin".
But less and less remains of what was real . . . '

4

Three, four, five mornings more,
Misted, half-warm, half-cold
Have drawn a half-sister to her.
Jointly they munch and flick
Their ears, their tails at flies,
Linked in a mute communion
Which both accepts and defies
The mutable border zone, their condition,
The given, taken, not to be gauged or told.

5

On the sixth morning her day-bed is bare.

At the ten-acre field's far end
These dots of colours that shift and blur
Against the hazed horizon must be cattle, grazing.

PLUM

Polymorphous from sloe
Through damson, bullace, pershore
To fleshy Victoria, exquisite gage,
If cousin to a canonical fruit,
Twelve times removed, it does not care:
Genealogy leaves it cold
As a freezer. But, philoprogenitive too,
Round or oval, it romps through colours,
Clouded dark-blue, purple to pink,
Goldenest yellow, green, variegations;
Puts out suckers all over the place
Yet will inbreed, interbreed,
The coarse with the highly cultured,
Unless grafted, restrained,
Dependent shamelessly
On its winged marriage brokers.

When the wingless claim reward
For the bother of ownership,
Selection, training, hygiene,
It hides from these predators,
In aerial loops evades
The picker bag wired to a stick,
Not ripe or caught till half-eaten,
Therefore discarded, disdained,
Escaping once more, to rot –
Down to the fertile stone
Which may raise again, anywhere,
Who knows what progeny, wilder;

And this, the random tree,
Once risen, may turn ascetic,
Thwart with mere leafage unnamed
The lust of curiosity.

IMPERTINENT QUESTIONS

(Postscript to 'Plum')

How many times removed
Over centuries for sure
If not millennia, Marvell's
Half-peach, his Nectaren
Plum-skinned, the velvet shed?
A hybrid cousin or
Pretender mimicking
The clan, its pale blood other?
Leave one enigma pure.
This human sister, brother –
What's their affinity
Beyond the family tree?

BEECH HEDGE IN WINTER

Roots cramped, boughs crippled,
Wherever minimal rays
Could reach its mass unbroken
It outlives the Lombardy poplar,
Most towering of the tall
That, planted here, stood free –
Laid low by hurricane.
Now stunted nurse to the hale,
Shelter to progeny,
Keeps what remains a garden.
Showing extractions, holed,
Still in drizzle, drabbest light,
Younger evergreens blackish,
Matt the lawn's perennial grass,
Brightly its darkness glows,
Barring no vistas, focus
For eyes as old,
A red unquenchable
Retained in its dead leaves
Till the budding push out the brittle;
And, cut once more into shape
Will close the gaps of decay.

MARROW

No name, description, warning
On the seed packet prepared us
For this, that as never before
Musically this plant would wind,
A twisted jungle creeper.
One stalk trailing away
Into the dark of apple foliage,
Like music it misled
With a wealth of sterile flowers.
Not one, close to the root,
Ground bass or nucleus
Foreknown, awaited, recalled,
Until very late was formed,
Then air-borne, little at that.
Had it been left to swell,
Inflate romantically,
Despite these delicate tendrils
Put out for climbing, clinging
Down it would have crashed,
The bulkier, the sooner to rot.
Attend! Attend! was all,
Search! Search for the fruit
To hide which the leaves expand.

ADVICE TOWARDS CLOSING TIME

If to yourself you sing
Through street and market clatter,
Inaudible – no matter.
For, flattered or ignored,
At best our best songs bring
Distraction to the bored.
It is the ending
Which they applaud:
An end to the pretending
That they were rapt or awed.
Before senescence does, forget the fuss,
Know that your true name is Anonymous
And always we're so many
That few of us are any
Save while a random lens picks out a face
Which, randomly too, another will replace.
Then, perhaps, faceless, dead,
You'll sing from silence beyond the silence shed.

WAITING FOR THE RIVER FERRY

Was there ever a bridge here?
A narrow one, light one at best,
Not for these tourist cars, nor commercial trucks,
Pontoons perhaps for war,
The ground either side too marshy always,
The bed always shifting, silted.
To swim it was more likely,
Weapons, provision left behind.

On the other bank, as on this,
Willows in clumps or single,
Rushes, reeds more amply renewed;
Cottages durably built
By labourers long redundant.
The names are different, two counties diverge,
Commingled in us who wait,
Weather and water growing more actual
Than routes, than destinations,
Till it matters least of all
Whether we cross or turn back.

A CAT'S LAST SUMMER

Still the warblers forage, in silence,
In myrtle fragrance as August turns autumnal.

Day after day she sits
On the same patch of grass,
Her senses waning, the well-deep eyes enlarged
But not for seeing,
Her needle-sharp hearing blunted;
And Belsen-thin, ribs showing through,
So fearless now that when a cock pheasant
Struts at her, clucking, claims the terrain,
She neither deigns to flee
Nor make to spring, as she could,
Agile enough, did a will impel her.

What she forgets is domesticity
And that affection paid
To nursing landlords, servant caterers
Whom by log fire, lamplight she sought out
For comfort, for their fondling,
Joined in their music, tail beating time, her time,
Bore with in electronic would-be worlds –
Lost to her now, receded
Like their, her house that briefly she'll re-enter
Only to feed and, running, at once abandon
For her true home, the myrtle-scented season
Holding her yet, while she
Dies back as leaves do from the living tree.

NOVEMBER LIGHT

Winds in abeyance, the sky swept clear,
More richly than kindling these embers shine,
Lessening days fulfilled,
Cock pheasant colours the shoot has missed.

Before its bareness the purple maple pales
To a vermilion-pink,
Cloud-rims come down to earth,
Before the russet that lasts all winter
Beech to a yellow-gold,
Half-deathly abundance released from need:
Ripe apples on leafless boughs,
Berries, the scarlet, the black,
Rose-hips at odds with time,
Not stripped yet by hunger in dearth –
Although drawn inland from woods and heath
The smaller birds return,
Deer venture nearer, one hare
Has braved a hedgerow to browse
Held in suspense, the year's
While mild as moonbeams the sun's rays linger,
Seem to mix in few shadows, blur no shape,
Leave this late gentian blue.

IV

CHIAROSCURO

Not for us this nightfall lingering,
Largesse of broken light
Filling the flatland sky
From western to eastern horizon
With colours that, earthly, would be of blood,
Coccus, verdigris, flower,
Chrysoprase, turquoise, malachite;
Such radiance above each road
As we drive home from another parting,
Sudden departure, one-way,
Dazzled, I do not see
What small mammal runs there for safety,
The headlight beams, dipped or undipped,
Listlessly blink, outshone.

Hazed, the new morning rays,
February's, from clouds deflect
Eyes to their every day,
For lesser illumination
Dot the pale foreground, foreknown:
Rime on the black ewe's fleece
Glistening white where overnight she has rested
On pasture marked for reversion to meadow.

AMOR FATI, FEBRUARY

1

Dead or alive it stands in the water-logged garden,
This gage-tree called Early Transparent
Next to the greengage favoured since I was young:
Fondly pushed flush into place
When one blast of a gale, northwesterly,
Left the base three quarters split,
Limbs loose or leaning, our footpath obstructed,
An upright tree bowed with its bulk;
Lopped then, staked and roped,
Tugged at once more by winds
And bare while scud contends with the morning sun,
Cold air with celandine opening, plum blossom clustered.

Yes, I weighed up the odds, acknowledged,
Yet another terminal case:
Had the wound been clean,
The hinging fibre sound,
Uprooted the trunk would have been, not cleft.

2

And knew that the zigzagging godlings,
The spiralling godlingesses
Who as understudies waited for ages
Now take the curtain calls,
In their green rooms wisecrack, brag.

Put away your straight lines,
Immaculate circle, spheres,
Equilateral triangle never in nature,
Probability's pros and cons,
Your cause and effect, means and ends, your stasis-
    cum-progression –
Toys of the dream of reason;
And these bones may live, they jeer, when the surgeon's
    buried
Under eccentric orbits of guessed at invisible stars.

3

In stillness returned, in storms preparing,
Constant uncertainty's grace
I leave it to mend or moulder;
Doddering back to the last from labour
Shall laugh, too, if memory's palate, inventive,
Savours again this freckled fruit.

CONVERSATION WITH THE MUSE
OF OLD AGE

... Oh, I believe them, darling, when they say
Your mother's maiden name was Mnemosyne.
Was it at her or your twin sister's funeral –
'Fibby', to me, but I mean Fantasy's –
That I was stricken not with grief but fleas?
She was the more admired,
I flirted with her till of her tales too tall,
Charm too cosmetic, I grew sick and tired
And you, Amnesia, became my one and all.

Yes, still the relics of a life encumber
My house, wild archive, jumbled head with lumber.
The more you visit me, the less I care
When I can't find that notebook entry anywhere:
If lost, mislaid, it wasn't worth the search.
Trivia it is that leave us in the lurch,
Being so many, as our needs grow fewer.
But when the table's bare
And appetite too weary to compare,
Old bones can make a feast of plainest fare.
Often I've thought abstention would be truer
To your condition, who never speak one word,
Sensing that you concurred ...
And yet, and yet
Somehow once more we've met,
Your message, mute: 'To serve me is to doubt.
Even from me
Take only flashes, hints of certainty –
Or on the roundabout
With slyer fools and liars you'll be spun.

Be slow enough, and as to everyone
Silence will come to you, a stillness enter
Residual movement, from the hidden centre –'

You, always you, when at odd hours we meet,
Named or unnamed I know the ten thousand things
Of wilderness, garden, office, workshop, street,
Present or obsolete,
I grope towards for song, for stutterings:
Once gathered, seen or heard,
Beyond occasion now they have occurred.

Diminished, numbed, estranged,
What's quite redundant is the spectre 'I'
Among companions dead or fled or fleeing
Unless in you again they have their being,
Re-selfed and rearranged.
So bless me with your blankness till I die.

AVOIR DE LA BOUTEILLE

Who was it, long ago, taught me this phrase
And made it stick, before my hearing blunted,
My memory was a junk shop, cluttered up?
Neat metaphor did it seem, this vintage idiom
Without a label, grown anonymous,
When wine, the new, the mellow, still came pure
As the first light of morning?

Now corked I rise from sleep,
A bitterness on the palate, on the tongue,
A sourness in the bloodstream, as in the air
Of every communal day.
Senescence? Worse, the knowledge
Of that our grandchildren will never taste,
Their very infancy adulterated.

To a Frenchwoman 'j'ai de la bouteille'
I tried, by mere extension
From tales to their re-teller, both gone stale:
Blankly she looked at me.
Our gabbled, garbled languages too are failing
And plastic-sealed in plastic bottles only
Will circulate for quick redundancy.
'Corked?' What was that? Could drink be made for keeping?
Vieux-jeu for sure, old hat not even funny.

Ah, but where new economies inflate,
Usage and use are cloyed,
The least of things, if durable, grows precious,
Dusted and washed, the glass long empty shines.

TAUTOLOGICAL ODE TO A CAT

Wise in your way, your ways, even before
In cat years you were old,
Put away kittenish things
But for a twitch at the faint sound of wings,
Small rustling in the grass,
You'll not read this and set no store
By words we mouth at you to lure or scold,
Cajole or flatter you, but let them pass,
Impervious, although
You've learned to heed the sharp word 'No!'
When you prepare
A leap to bedstead, table, chair
Or, worse, to the unwelcoming knees
Of one your pleasure would not please.

What of it? Long, throughout these years
I've written verses for noise-clotted ears.
Yours are much finer, your very silences true
To your own needs and nature, what you are and do –
Which here I will not shame
With the pretence
Of an identity that would make you mine,
Contagion of a human name,
Your age, sex, colour, place of residence,
Your status, provenance, genealogical line.

If poems had a topic,
Censors would say that mine is misanthropic.
Hissing, you'd disagree,
Gently would slap them with a padded paw,

Moved by a feline loyalty
More ancient than Mosaic-Roman law.
Oh, yes, you're useless, a notorious loner
Unfit for labour and obeying,
Congenitally free
Of purblind purpose, futile utility.
You roam and home as music does, conveying
A precious lesson to the host
Who'd use you, lord it as your owner:
Him, her you profit most.

Enough that, different, we have lived together
Contending with deregulated weather,
Domestic, local, national, world-wide.
Indifferent, do your still unfathomed eyes protest?
Often, but side by side
In a communion unexpressed
As first and last things will remain
While, arrogant, we meddle, fuss, explain.
Yes, yes, my verses will not purr or mew,
Nor caterwaul – their diction neutered,
Plainer than plain and not accoutred
With lush libidinizing rhetoric
You would not growl at now, left cold by every trick –

Now beast, now animal, numen coldly dear,
When musing, intimately chaste,
Never far off and never wholly near,
No song of mine will reach you. The less waste!
Sea water I've embraced,
Scaled rock, shaped wood, from soil drawn flowerhead,
Told the day's light, day-darkness too,
The mutable air above,

Conversed with blackbird, translated peacock, dove,
Praised making not usurious, mere daily bread,
Answered what is unanswering, like you.

Should I outlive you, not again I'll write
Plaintive commemoration, as I did before,
But let you roam into another night
In which you may see more
Than ever I could with diurnal eyes.
In kind your essence lies
And what I said
Of one, if right, to all of you applies,
Living or dead;
In darkness as in sunlight leave you wise.

CHAUFFEUSE

I was in London again,
Jefferies' jungle of steel, stone, brick
Reverting to sludge and slime,
Gissing's whirlpool of lonely schemers dragged down;
And there had been abandoned
By her who'd been home to me wherever we lodged.
Indifferent, I doled in digs,
Bare of ambition, a drop-out from the games.

Suddenly I remembered:
Somewhere there was a house
That must be mine still, neither sold nor let
When, decades ago, we left it,
Moved from residual woodland back to London –
Half-ruin – I could see it – grown Gothic in decay
Though mere Victorian Gothic it had pretended to
When with its servants' quarters we made do.
Now dereliction had laid bare
Magnificence beyond all means and use
Of lines and colours loosed, looming in wilderness
Islanded now on its Berkshire hill
Marked out by speculators even then
For their development, suburban and subrural.

So maimed, diminished, could I return there,
Defying means and use?
With colleagues dead or estranged I weighed the odds.
One of them read me a chapter from a book he planned
Proving that what most fervently I'd worked on always
Had been the worst of my aberrations.

I laughed at that, still capable of laughter,
Then harped again on the crux:
'She's left me, who was my chauffeuse.'
It was another's turn to laugh.
Dream is a punster. Never I'd uttered that word.
Yes, true, my driver, after I'd ceased to drive,
And she who kept me warm –
A fireside seat, as well, a dictionary tells me,
In some domestic parlance, lost, my hearth;
Beyond it, metaphrased,
Motor itself to me, heart of me, anima, muse.

One word's short-circuit cracked me back into time,
Wiped out the house, demolished when we were young,
Built again, dream laid on dream, by the need relived.

FRAGMENT

This dream site, who knows where,
With debris so mixed was littered –
Potsherds with pomp, culture's detritus with nature's –
That scholar, merchant scavengers had ceased
To stoop, search, sift for gain or vanity,
For hoarding or display.

At random there I lifted
The first thing stumbled on
Among the many scattered:
Coaxed from hard rock left rough
An old man's bearded face,
Features and work at one in fine defiance
Shaming the urge to trace
Either across millennia to a name,
Tendency, function which, while current, mattered.

A laughing voice: 'You bother with such stuff?
Mere earthenware that must revert to earth.'

Stone was the one reply,
A silence turned towards the questioner's eye,
Hint of intrinsic worth
If in live sunlight those dead features glittered.

APPENDIX TO THE DEEDS

Do gardeners, aged, count in flowers
Days, hours, the decades passed
Or moments, measureless, when surprise
Like children's primed their eyes?
If flesh were grass, well-rooted, self-seeded
Heedless it could outlast
The rare exquisite lost,
Hurricane-tossed, blighted,
Names as exquisite, all mixed up, benighted.
Steadfast, it's weeds that return
To make and mark a season
Now that no weather is true,
Cloud-blocked, cloud-swept or fine.
Together here they grew
The greater and the lesser celandine
Restricted but allowed
No less than cultivar
From aconite, sudden, to lingering nerine,
Corn, opium poppies dormant year after year
Until, the soil dug, richly they reappear,
Released again, running wild;
Hazed sky-blue: forget-me-not,
Behind it, columbine,
Multicolours hybrid but reaching back
To its alpine purple-black,
While honesty, seed medals massed for war,
Turned weed with a vengeance, by being stronger
And more than hinted at the gist:
Diversity of kind, shade, shape beyond

Encyclopedic, classifying list,
Unique every petal, frond,
One flora-bearing Earth – or none.
Since when? Till when? they ask no longer,
Beginnings, ends now far from them, too far.

SNOWED IN

Bare trees, bare shrubs in blossom,
Far off, on the water meadow,
The air turned whitish too,
Swans camouflaged to the point
Of perfection, invisible,
While hunger compels
The little dark muntjac deer
To trespass on hedged lawns –
Exposed, their eyes dazzled
When the sun's rays erupt,
Flashing in so much white,
Their wary ways fluffed.

2

But for milkman, laundryman
Who braved the lane cut off,
Slushed and iced into stillness,
No lesser white intrudes,
Newspaper, post suspended.
What moves is the wind,
Cloud-mass now thick, now broken,
Small birds astir to shake
Flake-laden twiglets, foraging;
And, beyond the snow's dominion,
Glib tongues as ever wagging
Of their need for so-called war.

3

It is the housed and fuelled
Who feel, suffer such need:
One oil-well craves another,
Then more and more, then all.
Snowed in, the Eskimo
Made their ice age suffice,
Snow-warmed like polar bear,
Most humanly could laugh.
White peace, white poetry
Flowered in that cruel light –
Till even they were pampered,
Manned the machines of greed.

4

Eaves, branches dripping now
Have pushed the newspaper home,
With it, the chill that numbs,
Our normality, thawing.

TRANSITION

On my own bed and she on hers beside it
From nightmare I woke into calm more uncanny,
Farther from me than my long departed her face.
A different light, not of the sun or moon
Suffused a space beyond recollection,
Inherent light, it seemed, yellowish overall.
If a green, blue, red dared mix in, it was merged
In shapes without shadows, mass without contour or kind,
So that wide awake as I was, I could not look
For the once nearest, most known –
All dissolved, my landmarks and ways,
The bounded ground of our tending,
Lifetime furniture put away into store.
Good riddance, blurred rockface gloated,
Here nobody, nothing, is mourned.
Only in this, a light so estranging, so still
Will you stir again to a meeting, mended by loss.

AVE ATQUE VALE

Moments remain, the sculpted, painted, drawn
Split second millennia long,
Current word silenced, ambered into song
Where nothing can change, no bee molest these petals
Which, met, undo me, leave me unborn or dead,
Unable to compare,
Let hand, make memory meddle.
Momentous did they seem? Not now, so still.
They are, are, are, are, are, the things I see
And will be when they're lost, obliterated,
The model passed away.
On this old empty vase glazed patterns dance,
Above it fixed wings beat, the migrants' flight.

Good morning, present, absent ones, good night.

Poetry by Michael Hamburger from Anvil

Collected Poems 1941–1994

A distinctive body of work, reflecting half a century's dedication to his art which has consistently engaged with both the natural and human worlds.

Late

A narrative meditation in a style akin to his 'Variations', *Late* is both an elegy for and a celebration of life towards the end of the millennium.

Intersections

A varied collection of his shorter poems written between 1994 and 1999, meditating on the intersections of past and present, of continuity and change.

A Diary of Non-Events

A year in the poet's life, blending observation of changes in the natural world with his daily life in and around his Suffolk home, as the larger concerns of the outside world intrude.

'Few English poets of our day can have come to their craft with the cultural and linguistic richness of Michael Hamburger ... a thoroughly European, even cosmopolitan sensibility who is at the same time a nature poet of thoroughly English stamp. A Brechtian social and political satirist co-exists, and not always peaceably, alongside a knowledgeable naturalist who dwells among the cloudscapes and birdsong of Suffolk ... As a translator, of course, but also as a distinctive, wide-ranging poet, Hamburger has been more than usually attentive to the divisions, to the "shocks and conflicts" of his century; his work helps us share in them, and enriches our understanding.'

STEPHEN ROMER, *Agenda*

Some German poetry from Anvil

TRANSLATED BY MICHAEL HAMBURGER

Paul Celan: Poems

'Through these exemplary translations the English reader can now enter the hermetic universe of a German-Jewish poet who made out of the anguish of his people, and his own representative sufferings, things of terror and beauty.'

Times Literary Supplement

Goethe: Roman Elegies
and other poems

This edition collects all Michael Hamburger's Goethe translations, including the complete *Roman Elegies*. His selection and introduction provide a valuable account of 'a writer so many-sided as to constitute a whole literature'.

Peter Huchel: The Garden of Theophrastus

The poetry of Peter Huchel (1903–1981) has its roots in Brandenburg, where his formative years were spent. Through the hardship of the Second World War and its vexed aftermath, culminating in his exile to West Germany in 1971, he maintained a poetry of humane commitment, formal invention and precision.

Rainer Maria Rilke: Turning-Point

Hamburger's choice of Rilke's miscellaneous poems from 1912 to his death in 1926 first appeared as *An Unofficial Rilke*. He argues that the 'workshop' poems have been underrated and that they are important to understanding Rilke.

'The collusion of Hamburger the German scholar and Hamburger the poet gives the translations what is for me an unrivalled distinction.'

MICHAEL HANKE, *PN Review*